# Keys to the Forest:

## A poetic journey

## By Tom George

### Illustrated by Jennie Wishart

Copyright © 2023 by Tom George

Heartwell Books

Copyright © 2023 by **Tom George**

All rights reserved. No part of this publication may be reproduced, distributed or transmitted in any form or by any means, without prior written permission.
**Heartwell Books**

Illustrations by Jennie Wishart

**Keys to the Forest/ Tom George**
ISBN 978-1-7393737-0-2

To all

"At the same time that we are earnest to explore and learn all things, we require that all things be mysterious and unexplorable, that land and sea be indefinitely wild, unsurveyed and unfathomed by us…"

**- Henry David Thoreau**

# Contents

Autumn.................................................13

Seen and Unseen...................................14

Lana's Pen.............................................17

Like a Poem...........................................19

Match of the Day...................................21

Green and Black....................................23

A Smile on the Bus................................25

Street Sweeper......................................28

The Other Side of the Wall....................33

Cold Dark Morning................................37

Sweet Charity........................................41

Library Life.............................................47

Continuum.............................................54

Lost and Found.....................................58

Dream Upon Dream..............................62

Call of the Wild......................................65

River Man..............................................68

Heartwood.............................................73

At This Moment.....................................76

The Green Man.....................................81

Permission to Live.................................85

Weed World...........................................89

Groundling................................................96
Inner Vision........…......................................99

Acknowledgements............…..........................103
About the author.......................................105

## Autumn

A small boy kicks up leaves on a suburban street. It is a cold autumn day and he has been stuffed into a set of warm clothes. The dry leaves make an exciting crispy sound and he can't resist stamping, kicking and wading through them. There are also wet patches where the leaves have been trodden so much that they squish under his feet.

*"watch out for the dog poo!"* a concerned parent calls.

The cold air is not kind to soft cheeks and noses, but autumn brings the loving warmth of planned outings and gatherings, bolstering against the cold with collective effort, setting out on woodland walks with dogs, clustering round bonfires waving sparklers and throwing sticks high into conker trees to dislodge spiky green treasures.

In the park, the trees have transformed from green to golden yellow, rusty tones and crimson; devastating beauty reflected in the still water of the lake. Nature is slowing down, preparing for a long sleep. The child frolics, but the parent feels a poignancy; the sadness of light reducing, nature echoing the cycle of human life, teaching the necessity of treasuring important moments and letting other things pass.

**Seen and Unseen**

I come here almost every day

and stay a little while

I'm someone that you recognise

you nod your head and smile

and although you acknowledge me

there's something plainly true

you've never really seen me

and I've never seen you

Despite the daily greeting

and superficial smiles

the distance that's between us

could be a thousand miles

We keep the interaction

as breezy as can be

I've never really seen you

and you've never seen me


For what goes on behind the face

remains the great unknown

the landscape of our inner lives

is never truly shown

Each and every human heart

remains a secret world

a tightly rolled up document

that rarely gets unfurled


People come here regularly

to while away their time

interacting calmly, as if the weather's fine

but underneath the carapace

what kind of storms are blowing?

is the pressure mounting high

with cruel skies ever-snowing?

We still go through the motions

as we pass every day

keeping friendly boundaries

giving nothing much away

the inner complications

never leaking through

you've never really seen me

and I've never seen you

**Lana's Pen**

When we met up today

you lent me a pen

to write something down


It's stayed with me somehow

and as I hold it in my hand

it seems to reflect something of you


Modest and practical, it gets a job done

a pure blue for a purity of spirit,

like a clear sky on a cold fresh day

when you might be out taking a walk


I'll see you soon

and I'll return it

from one writer

to another

...and back again


*Lana Brady (1933-2011)*

*Folk singer, writer and mother of seven. Achieved a B.A. Hons in Creative Writing in 2007 at the age of 74, the oldest student ever to graduate from Liverpool John Moores University.*

**Like a Poem**

I'm in like with you

It's a big thing to say

But I knew it for sure

On our first day

I waited for you to accept my request

You must have liked me – did I look at my best?

Whenever I post a comment or pic

You like it first, you're always so quick.

But is this true like

Or something lightweight?

I wouldn't want like to turn into hate

Whatever you share with me

I will approve

I live to commend your every move

It's so addictive this like that we've found

Just look and you'll see - like is all around

Like is a four-letter word with no risk,

Pleasantly positive, hard to resist

Let's continue this like affair

While it feels fresh

And maybe one day

We'll meet in the flesh

**Match of The Day**

Cradled on my Dad's lap

rocked by the rise and fall of his chest

a wash of grey noise from a black and white TV

a crowd is calling, voices soaring

Match of the Day

A throaty swell

That ebbs and flows

Roiling and crashing

Like waves on a beach

as I dip to sweet oblivion

then surface to the glow

of staying up late

and manful meaning

Dad's chest and shirt-neck smell

occasional jolts as his whole body clenches

and he urges "Go on!" to the figures on the screen

then notices I am no longer watching

surrenders to duty

and carries me upstairs

## Green and Black

Sometimes on weekends, Dad would come into the house with oily black hands, after working on the car outside. Opening the cupboard under the sink, he would take out a squat red tin bearing the legend *Swarfega*. After the careful torsion of his oily hands on the screw thread top, the magical substance would be revealed - glowing green with a thrilling chemical smell, still bearing the finger scoops from last time.

Standing next to him with my chin on the edge of the sink, I would watch fascinated as Dad sank his fingers into the thick-set goo, pawed out a palmful and set to work, covering his hands with an expert methodical motion, the wrists turning and fingers mingling, each hand massaging the other, green merging with black as he patiently worked the oil free.

How had he learned this? I wonder if he had watched his father, who died before I was born. Did he observe the same process; unhurried hands entwining in a necessary but meditative chore, a ritual delineating work and rest, as if washing off hours of effort and concentration; the oily grey water escaping down the plughole.

After rinsing, time for another palmful, the hands are returning to pink and now Dad attends to the oil that persists in the familiar gnarls of his knuckles.

I am not allowed to dip my fingers in, but occasionally,

in a secret transgression, I creep into the empty kitchen and unscrew the lid myself for a furtive look and sniff the zingy, petrochemical fragrance contained within. My time will come. Before long I will be introduced to the secrets of bike maintenance. I too, will be anointed with oil and then get to partake in the same purification ritual using Swarfega - the precious substance.

## A Smile on The Bus

Somebody left a smile on the bus

And nobody noticed but me

Lying on the seat

Blissful and complete

Waiting for someone to see


While it lay there

People were looking elsewhere

Staring though grimy glass

At the dregs of the day

Or lost in flashing screens

United in separation

Desire and complication


The smile was within easy reach

Orphaned but happy

Self-contained

Unrestrained

Needing nothing to sustain

Or even explain

Its ever-emerging warmth

And wordless wisdom


I picked up the smile

And tried it for size

I felt like a new born boy

It suited me fine

Had always been mine

I'd simply forgotten my joy


Like a travelling seed

Or a windblown spore

A smile will propagate

And make many more


Gently unlocking

The innermost light

Spreading its message

Of secret delight

And precious insight


Would you donate a smile

To someone who needs it?

Afterwards you get a cup of tea

And a biscuit


Or maybe just leave one in a public place

Without any fuss

It would not be so bad

If from time to time

We all left smiles on the bus

**Street Sweeper**

Under skies of pigeon grey

drifting on the winds

you left Dubrovnik for a new beginning

now you sweep up the ends of things


The well-sucked fag butts

and ice lolly sticks

your cart filling up with ghosts

empty shells of revelries

or antidotes to woes


Feeding your cuckoo cart

that always wants more

seeking out the bounty

of your ongoing war

Life can be so simple

just obeying orders

You lean into an eternal hill

and hope this way is forwards

After a storm, the drowning flags

chatelaines of evening lights

broken brollies dumped in doorways

Could be swatted flies


Sunday morning duties

the debris of the night

sweeping up the lost dignity

of long-gone, unknown tribes


A sequined bowler, hen night sash

mangled chips, a false eyelash


Drops of blood and vomit

conflicts now forgotten

battle scenes easily cleaned

and moved on from


Beer bottles sleeping in the gutter

are comrades lying innocently
Corporal Kravic steps over
gathers them in tenderly

Street sweeper, finder and keeper
humble treasures gleaned
a crystal necklace in your pocket
cradled and redeemed

Heading homeward, out of sight
your ears still ringing in the morning light
as, piece by piece, you find
peace of mind

*A few years ago, I was in central London, looking for the V&A without success. I saw a man emptying litter bins into a cart, so I went over and asked him for directions, but he paid no attention to me, either not hearing or not understanding; or not wanting to do either. He was a white man in his 40s and had a thick 'Slavic' moustache.*

*'He probably gets sick of being asked for directions' I told myself, at the same time as feeling a bit miffed. But I wondered about him*

*and where he had come from. The Bosnian war was still comparatively recent history and I imagined him fleeing the ruins of his former life there.*

*I guess it's more likely that he was Polish, but who knows? This poem came out of it. A few years further on, the invasion of Ukraine by Russia created trauma on the Eastern edge of Europe once more and the poem seemed to resonate again.*

**The Other Side of The Wall**

There will be no more divisions

No cultural collisions

Or blinkered racial visions

On the other side of the wall


There will be no flagellations

No female mutilations

Or power-hungry nations

With no mercy at all


There won't be terror forces

Denial of resources

Or distant bearded voices

With stony holy vows


No vicious circle game

Of here we go again

Where history takes the blame

But punishment is now

On the other side of the wall

The strong will heed the call

Of dignity for all

The need to understand

To heal the great divide

The festers deep inside

And cannot be denied

When written on the land

On broken Belfast streets

Where concrete keep the peace

With reinforced beliefs

That stand twenty feet tall

In East and West Berlin

The long-divided kin

Who never did give in

Until they saw it fall

In Gaza's battered strip

Where sniper bullets rip

A nation in the grip

Of merciless control

Existing without power

Beneath the lookout tower

With murder by the hour

And hospitals in holes

On the other side of this pain

Truth will fall like rain

And pour down onto flame

Extinguishing the grief

On the other side of this rage

The troops will disengage

Like someone turned a page

Restoring our belief

There will be no more excuses

No temporary truces

Or human rights abuses

To dim the inner light

Suspicion will be banned

And martyrs will be slammed

And people will demand

Their safety from the fight

On the other side of the wall

Hearts run free

Horizons of hope

Stretch continuously

The dream of all nations

Believe it we must

On the other side of the wall

The rebirth of trust

**Cold Dark Morning**

It was a dark December morning

that coldly came to pass

with black outside the windows

and frost upon the glass

The kitchen taps were weeping

the air itself was numb

and a certain sense of trauma

in my Daddy and my Mum

Keeping up the routine

in automatic ways

with voices so distracted

and eyes so clearly dazed

The news reports were blasting

with that infernal song

'Imagine there's no heaven…'

repeating on and on


December 1980 - a season without grace

who would have thought we'd finish up

at such a pointless place

Never has a decade slammed so cold into the face

to say an era's over and gone without a trace


And things that were the comfort

and the cushion of my world

now took on a faintly tragic air…


The lyrics to 'Imagine' in my mother's kindest hand

pinned up on the kitchen wall

or on a music stand

Daddy's Lennon glasses that went well with a smile

and all the vinyl albums in scuffed-up gatefold style

These things at once were over

archaic in a sense

speaking of an era consigned to the past tense


And still from every radio

that slow and stately song

recast as an elegy

playing ever long


It was a dark December morning

and I was ten years old

and my strangely silent parents

just couldn't be consoled


*The morning we woke to the news that John Lennon had been shot dead. Where were you when you heard?*

**Sweet Charity**

There's one on every high street

Sometimes four or five

Giving all their merchandise a second chance at life

Prepare for some surprises If you should make a stop

At this humble emporium - the charity shop


Browsing among oddities, gems and mysteries

Customers investigate, keen as honey bees

Flipping through the albums

searching through the racks

and scanning the selection of random bric-a-brac


a flashing plastic dalek, a garish 70s vase

a miniature piano, a pack of tarot cards

A paperweight from Margate, a cruet set with eyes

A statue of the Buddha looking very wise

Every item here knows the touch of human life

carries the vibration of love and hope and strife

here and there chips and cracks offering their clues

despite some imperfections, they still can be of use


Silk scarves lie entangled in an opened red suitcase

Elegant, alluring and reclining in disgrace

Woolen overcoats packed in tightly on a rail

Like a line of dockers queueing outside in the hail


Nearly-new walking boots next to power heels

Pose before the mirror - test and try the feel

Walking in the imprints of someone else's feet

An eerie intimacy with someone you'll never meet


The crew of this establishment

are all doing their best

All efforts appreciated - they're not under duress

Once, they ventured through the door

keen to be of use

With skills to offer charity or nothing much to lose


There's Alison the student, doing social work exams

Tom the young guitarist, who wants to join a band

Daniel, from Uganda, who's hoping he can stay

and Brenda every Monday

who's just lost husband Ray

Everyone is welcome to donate time and care

Help out in the background or demonstrate their flair

Chatting to the customers or sorting through the junk

The treasures and monstrosities

thick with dust and gunk


Bin liners and boxes constantly arrive

Carrying their secrets, capsules of lost lives

Deposited by relatives when Mum goes in the home

Or downsizing retirees

whose offspring now have flown


Stacks of Jackie Collins, Jeffrey Archer

and Dean Koontz

Next to Penguin classics and sumptuous art books

All life co-existing, epic contrasts of taste

All can be attractive and rarely go to waste


This could be the very place to find that new costume

For those who like a bargain and don't over-consume

Each item has a secret past, it's future can be yours

And don't you love that feeling

of supporting a good cause?

## Library Life

Liverpool Central Library is a haven, a cerebral sanctuary that you reach in relief after traversing the city centre, with its unrelenting consumerist messaging. Flanked by its neighbors the gallery and museum, this neo-classical edifice embodies a proud civic tradition, welcoming all who cross its threshold: students, schoolkids, seekers and searchers, the retired, the inspired, the homeless and tired, trainees, refugees, the oddly-dressed and quite obsessed...

A librarian looks up wistfully at the imposing structure. After a lifetime of service within, one last shift remains. Over decades of quiet, careful duty, oceans of thought have passed through these hands; the books coming and going in overlapping tides, venturing out across the city on intrepid journeys, to be caressed by hands of strangers, gradually losing their pristine innocence; returning, sometimes scarred, to roost on shelves, tightly packed, keeping the secrets of the lives they have touched.

The librarians are an endangered species. With the ever-advancing decades, these humble civic servants, often raised in the age of the page, have had to become computer whisperers and printer midwives. The wistful librarian remembers stamping dates in the inside covers by hand; the dates building up, as in a well-travelled passport; pictures the little wooden drawers full of catalogue cards, recalls the parquet floor that squeaked under the shoes, before the tide of carpet washed in.

Oh yes, before they renovated. Ten years ago, on orders from above, fluorescent men ripped out the old guts of the building and poured in the budgets of a dozen cancelled local libraries. A miraculous new vision rose from the hole. A computerised confection of steel, glass and timber, sitting inside the neo-classical shell. A dream of openness, light and liberty ascending and breaking out through the roof.


An invasion of scamps

Play chase among the shelves

Intoxicated by youth

And an overdose of Now

The silence is a fresh white canvas for their shrieks

Running for the door

As the security guard approaches


Up on the second floor, the man who sits all day reading car manuals has found a companion who looks at road maps. They came together from opposite sides of the library; now they sit side by side and make sense of the world. Downstairs in the cafe, a study group has convened to discuss Vedic literature. Esoteric phrases decorate the air, interrupted by the screams of the tea urn. Sanskrit words issue from mouths inbetween slurpings of flat whites and 'squirty cream'-topped hot chocolate.

At the main desk stands the wistful librarian. A man approaches.

MAN: It's amazing what they've done with this place innit? Beautiful…it needed doing up, mind. I've been coming here fifty-odd years.

LIBRARIAN: So have I…

MAN: I used to come here as a young man, on me days off, read the newspapers, find out what was going on in the world, you know. We didn't have a telly or anything like that. But I had this thirst for knowledge, and it was all here…this was the world. I haven't been to university or anything like that, but this place opened up me mind, you know?

LIBRARIAN: That's good to hear. A lot of people tell me that.

MAN: A lot of people our age, they just give up don't they? Not me. I'm doing research into me family tree, going back hundreds of years. That's what's in here. *(pats a folder)*

LIBRARIAN: Have you found the archives?

MAN: Yeah, but I've got to go home now and feed the dog…you know, some of these young ones, they don't know they're born, they don't appreciate places like this. Look at that lot, messing about *(indicates a group of school kids*)…it drives me mad. You see, in our day we had nothing. No phones or iPhones or whatever they have these days, and we were glad of any opportunity to learn.

LIBRARIAN: They usually settle down eventually. To be honest, in this job you learn to take it all in your stride. You have to.

MAN: You seem very chilled out. Come to think of it, I've never seen an angry librarian.

LIBRARIAN: Oh, you'd be surprised…

(A young girl approaches)

GIRL: Have you got any books on slavery?

LIBRARIAN: Yes, you want the history section. Go around to the right and you'll find all the slavery books there.

In the vast circular reading room, kept and restored, a noble tradition of quiet study is miraculously maintained. Scholars sit in deep absorption while the domed ceiling throws back their minutest shuffling sounds in pristine echoes. Awestruck tourists creep in and their cameras emit soft digital clicks. By the door, an interactive touchscreen display relates the history of the building…*Established by William Brown in 1860….designed by Thomas Allom*…waistcoated gentlemen posing with pride.

On a continuous ring of shelving three stories high,

huge leather-bound volumes sit humming with thought. Accessible by a perilous network of walkways and spiral staircases, the accumulated global knowledge of the Victorians. These volumes, sleeping so inscrutably, are as alive as ever, their voices preserved in the magical technology of print. If opened at random, tropical birds fly out, ancient armies roar, steam engines hiss, gothic cathedrals soar to the heavens, histories of disease spill onto the floor, clouds of philosophy hang enigmatically...

And among all of this

As busy as ants

Wiping the tables

And picking up cans

Everyday angels with blue latex hands

De-greasing the keyboards

And freshening the air

Removing the chewy

And coffee stains

Of library lifers

With itching brains

Who stay in later if it rains

But not allowed to doze and drool

For this is now

A flagship jewel

**Continuum**

Silent spiral messenger

from distant ages past

roused from ancient bed rock

washed up behind glass

Your secrets locked in sediment

through dark ages of night

now to be deciphered

in scientific light


Like some primeval motor

with spark as yet unseen

riding the momentum

of evolution's scheme

All life spinning outwards

to manifest and flower

the manifold emergence

of Gaia's quiet power

High above your cemeteries

heaving tumult seas

sultry ocean currents

brewing vortices

Whirling ever faster

like saw mill blades unmoored

promising disaster

when landfall is assured


Experts in the weather rooms

modelling the paths

grappling with data

salvation via maths

The technocratic mission

of reason and control

built on burning fossils

and snuffing out the soul


Turning, ever turning

the dark within the light

with certainty a stranger
and reason out of sight
Find the silent centre
within the whirling mass
as narratives unravel
and edifices crash

Basking under halogen
the ammonite displayed
a mineral memorial
from life's endless parade
A temporary stranger
the seabed's honoured guest
that whirled for an eternity
and came at last to rest

That mesmerising pattern
too deep to understand
a permanent reminder
as oceans claim the land

That we have just this moment

to value what we see

but linked in a continuum

exist eternally

**Lost and Found**

You live by the sea

a few miles from me

and walk the shore

on a wind-whipped day

when the air is full of sky


Do you find things the tide no longer wants?

Do they have a still calmness

lying at infinite rest

stroked smooth

by the whole world ocean

lapping against them like a lullaby?


With the breath of the surf gasping in your shell-like

you tread the shore

looking through your mind's eye

at the edge of the land

The waves wash away worry

walk long enough and you find

that everything is like tracks in sand

Hey beachcomber

life gets matted sometimes

and stinks a bit

like bladderwrack

Tease it all out

with a sandy stride

then tell the tide

you have to get back


As a child my bravest castles

intrigued my architect Dad

on Newport beach

but it turned there was no maiden in the tower

no kingdom to be claimed

too much water in the bucket

Fuck it

Hey beachcomber

what's the point in disappointments?

we made it here

wherever we are


Gather up your orphan objects

a cast-off bracelet

a castaway key

Put them all in your bag of cameo stars

for your next production


The ocean is your neighbour

the waves don't need to explain

the sky is an open mind

the sand gives way gladly

And it's ok, beachcomber

I found a place with the lost and found things

I will see you on the mantelpiece

**Dream Upon Dream**

And in my dream of death

A moth landed on my arm

But it was your father

Who had recently passed

Gently, I placed him on the ground

He fell to dust

And was blown away on the wind


And in my dream of birth I was angry

I wasn't quite ready

I wanted seven more days

I'd spent so long planning this

My grand entrance

For you it was just nine months

But it was everything I knew


And in my dream of life

I walk among crowds of people

Lost among the multitudes

And I can't see where one person ends

And the next one begins

Dream upon dream

Intermingling like waves on the ocean

Dream upon dream

With no distance between


In this waking reality

Lost to our imaginings

We see only our projections

From moment to moment

We dream our very selves

And each others' intentions


Meet me tonight in our dream

In our world of infinite potential

There will be a park bench

Under the velvet sky

I will see you there

And we will plan our awakening

**Call of the Wild**

In your freer moments
your senses sharpen
attune to the scent
the fragrance that carries across the land
woodsmoke and heather
drifting in the wind

Restless spirit, uncover your essence
that speaks in the language of plants
find your keen purpose
and firm grounding
in wisdom and healing
with sure heart and noble poise

In your purer moments
the moonlight seems to call you
back to an ocean of knowing
written in the song of your cycles

deep care and the deep life

rooted in timeless flow


Sheltering heart, remember your presence

that shines in the truth of the moment

dancing the rapture of your love

with wide eyes and hot breath


In your truer moments

you trust the instinct

encoded in your bones

seeing what your instincts show

uncover the lessons

you already know


Gathering soul, as you become whole

taste the wildish nature

guiding you home

protecting your own

with soft fur and sharp teeth

**River Man**

Who is this man

Calm and still

Watching the river flowing

Crystal clear

Deep and strong

Effortlessly knowing

What has shaped him

nourished him

guided him

to this elemental quietude?

grounded thus

no phone, no fuss

unified in solitude

He has learnt the ageless lessons

that still the mind

and focus the heart

and calm the tongue


He feels the ground under naked feet

draws the air into his presence

all doubt falls silent

and listens


Friends may come

To taste the peace

The clarity

That glistens


If you ask him

what is a man?

He may simply smile

shaking out his dreadlock mane

no urge to explain

no doubts to disguise

he simply says, with patient eyes

*'Om Namah Shivaya'*

To calm your questing heart

Words are not

The place to start

Watch the breath

To still the mind

And soon enough

You too might find…

*This* man is

clear

Steady

Fluid

Patient

Focused

consistent

timeless




*Om Namah Shivaya (Sanskrit)*

"I honor the divinity within me."

**Heartwood**

Sing to me your heartwood song

a song without words

that can only be heard

with the third ear

that lies at the heart of a person

that knows itself in stillness

and finds itself in wildness


Tell me what I already know, deep soul

but forgot over lifetimes

about who we really are

and how it all happens


You live the slowest story

you teach the ancient, patient ways

passed on since the dawn of all days

you know so well - too much to tell

about the very root of being

Heartwood heartbeat

watcher of time

reaching down deeply

through sleep of stony loam

plumbing the depths of earth consciousness

passing up the riches of life force

In silent sap, that knows no hurry


Sing to me your heartwood song

slow and sure, deep and long

a song too deep to hear

with the mind's ear

those ancient bass notes of being

sung to the rhythm of seasons

inviting us to harmonise

and realise our reasons

**At This Moment**

At this moment

the sun burns bright

a cloud glows white

the air holds light

a bird makes flight

At this moment

the new blooms sing

the church bells ring

the trees lose doubt

the leaves reach out

At this moment

a grey form dies

a spirit flies

a sister cries

a stream runs wise

Can you hear the music inside the colours

that brings your spirit back to wellness?

At this moment

the shock waves grow

the wise don't know

the cruel winds blow

the torments show

At this moment

the systems crash

the heroes dash

the tempers break

foundations shake

At this moment

the anxious peace

the suspect breeze

infected space

we look for grace

At this moment

a lapwing calls

a dead branch falls

the lake lies deep

the old stones sleep


Can you feel the oneness within the stillness

that brings your being back to wholeness?


At this moment

the seagulls glide

the sky looks wide

a new life wakes

an old wound aches


At this moment

a new bud forms

the cold earth warms

a skylark strives

and hope arrives

At this moment

the perfumes drift

the evenings lift

the seasons shift

and life's a gift


At this moment




*Written in spring 2020 during the Covid lockdown*

## The Green Man

As a child I was told

don't be too bold

stick to the road safety plan

follow the code

when you cross the road

always watch for the green man


Green man, I'm waiting

holding Mum's hand

gazing with expectant eyes

trusting your shadow

to fill up with light

you always materialise


You're not wearing clothes

you don't have a nose

your flavour is probably lime

your strawberry mate

tells us to wait

or tempt bitter fate, down the line


You're the gate keeper, permission-giver

the silent, inscrutable boss

When your spirit glows humanity knows

you're alive and it's safe - we can cross


I've watched you for years, waiting for safety

stuck on this side of the road

But you're safe already

how do I get to the emerald realm that you know?


Green man, you're springtime, pleasantly warm

your spirit so vibrantly glows

Light filters through your chlorophyll form

healing, the way nature knows

The red man is paralysed

only sees risk

he only wants us to refrain

He's living in hell

he's glowing as well

hot with resistance and pain


When green appears

there is no doubt

discipline turns to release

This is the time

for confident strides

onwards to do as we please


I can see the road's clear

I want to be free

little green man

Where's the *you* within me?

Over the road is life unrestrained

a whole new day of fun

a park, the swings and innocent things

I'm holding on tight to Mum


Green man, you are life unchained, but I'm still learning what's real and what's safe. So, I take my fear and my pain out in the sun and rain where nature might somehow explain how things can just peacefully flow…


And if I go down to the woods today

I'll return to where I began

And if I look into the trees enough

I might just see the green man

**Permission to Live**

Permission to speak

It starts with the word

Who can express

Who's seen and not heard


Permission to feel

What's deepest within

To dare to expresses it

And not fear sin


Permission to love

Do you have to ask

Have you been waiting

As if it's a task?


Permission to heal

And see your own wealth

The simple permission

To love your true self


Permission - who gives it?

And who's to receive?

Who has the right

To choose, to believe?

Unconsciously, we wait for permission

Following old tracks, with clouded vision


Just allow it   …   Allow yourself   ….   Your Self


A smile is contagious

It welcomes the day

Your spirit leaks out

And shows others the way


You're casting aside

Those unwritten rules

That we never question

And follow like mules


When a dancefloor is bare

It takes a decision

For one to get up

And give all permission


To reach the far shore

And find what we lack

We must realise

What's holding us back


Awaiting permission

Our peace is proscribed

But what's disallowed and what's self-denied?

And who's permission do you actually need

To start a new life at a different speed?

I see many people

Stuck at the lights

Awaiting the signal

That lets them take flight


Frozen in profile

Awaiting permission

To finally move forward

And live their own vision

**Weed World**

This is for the weeds

the feral rebel seeds

that sprout without self-doubt

and have no interest in our needs


Defiantly they grow

dismissive of the hoe

and full of brazen confidence

they still put on a show


Invading garden borders

defying marching orders

infesting pavement cracks

resisting all attacks


Offensive to our goal

of coercive control

the anarchy of nature

reasserting its wild soul


This is for the pests

who make their nasty nests

And never seem to rest

pursuing new conquests


Feasting on our plants

oblivious to rants

determinedly they strive

to reproduce and thrive


The uninvited mice

the cockroaches and lice

infesting, never resting

and ignoring our advice


They find their comfort zones

within our very homes

they bury into tomes

and turn up on our combs


This is for the species

that found interesting niches

now targeted

'cos humans don't appreciate their features

They play their crucial part

in mother nature's art

but demonised as pestilence,

they're ordered to depart


For nature must be tamed

scientifically named

and if decreed unhelpful

then excluded and defamed

We tether and improve

and otherwise. remove

the carriers of life-force

of which we don't approve


This is for the breed

with insatiable need

proliferating globally

with exponential speed

They took over their planet

how carelessly they ran it

Devouring land and sea

For brute economy


This is for the beasts

who think ahead the least

focusing their brains

on maximising gains

The parasitic kind

who pay so little mind

to the web of co-existence

with which they are entwined

This is for the whole

where all can play a role

dandelion and ragwort

hornet, bat and mole

Where none is stigmatised

the balance is the prize

And what comes through, with patience

can delight and surprise

This is for the cast

of beings holding fast

to freedom of expression

despite being harassed

Singing ever-strong

their own authentic song

despite being informed

they're wrong and don't belong

This is for the life

that hustles to survive

that pushes through adversity

and somehow stays alive

Defiant of the trait

that wants to separate

everything we love

from everything we hate

## Groundling

Today I went to a place that is rather special to me – the pine forest at Formby. I'd been feeling a deep need to reconnect with wildness; and inspired by a friend, I did it without shoes.

As I enter the woods, I spontaneously greet the trees with a call that echoes across the undulating landscape; a gently descending slope of large dunes, covered with conifers, originally planted to prevent erosion. The trees are quite widely spaced, letting dappled sunlight in to the forest floor. Moss coats the ground, with brambles and ferns growing thickly in the hollows.

I climb to a high point and look down on the scene around me. It's late September but this evergreen world still feels fresh; sunlight twinkles off a million leaves and butterflies flirt here and there.

I sit down using my coat for a blanket underneath me. There is a stillness here that is almost tangible. I sit for a long time, bathed in warmth and green. Nothing is needed in this immersive re-connection. For my ears, there is only the faint rustle of the pines in the merest breath of breeze, the occasional bird call and the putter of a propeller aeroplane far overhead. And there is something else - the silence behind it all. Just *being* here is my meditation. Occasionally the distant ghost of something like a thought seeps into my consciousness, but finds no purchase and melts away.

I lie down and take my shoes and socks off; these feet are amazed at the shock of fresh air. Now horizontal, I find I am becoming part of the landscape for invertebrates. All around me, tiny spiders and ants are making their way through the micro-forest of moss and shoots and continuing their journeys over my hands and feet, up my back and into my hair.

I set off across the moss-covered dunes, savouring the soft natural carpet underfoot. My feet bend and flex according to the contours of the ground as they are meant to; gripping the slopes as I walk rather than just landing on them. It's as if my feet are remembering something that they hardly had a chance to learn in the first place. Walking barefoot is a natural sensory experience that we have deprived ourselves of since, who knows, a thousand years of footwear? Until very recently in much of the world, shoes were a rarity and a luxury. This connection with the Earth, taken for granted by human beings for millennia, has been lost within a few generations.

Of course, walking barefoot across the landscape is easy if your feet are used to it, but mine are lily-white and baby soft; locked up inside shoes for forty-odd years they have barely aged. But my enthusiasm knows no bounds; scrambling across the dunes I reconnect with abandon, grinning and wincing at the sharp twigs and brambles. A crimson scratch appears between my toes. I wonder how long it would take for my soles to remember their true purpose and toughen into feral leather.

I stop on a gentle slope covered with pristine moss. The pines end here and the sun floods in. Taking out a snack of sesame seeds and carrot sticks, I look out on an expanse of dense scrub with a sandy path that winds to the beach. I start to hear tiny impacts on the ground around me. Something is dropping from the tree above, small chips of vegetation. I reach for one; it's a fragment of nut casing. I look up and see a squirrel's tail twitching far above – dark red against the sky. Soon after, the squirrel discards the core of a pine cone, then another.

After lying down and meditating, I experience a strong breakthrough into present moment awareness. Everything is suddenly more sharp and real.

I curl myself around the trunk of a pine and don't move for ten minutes. Hugging a tree, one experiences a bottomless calm. These life forms are living on a very different timescale to us. They can teach us, but not in a way we can understand intellectually. I have heard that if you put your ear close to a tree you can sometimes hear it growing. I don't hear anything but the blood flowing through my ears - *my own* life force

I have no idea what time it is, but the sun is getting low in the sky and the breeze becoming fresher. Small birds start to appear in the trees around me, chatting to each other as they find their roosting spots. Formby, I hope you don't mind that I took some pine cones and sampled your blackberries. I'll be back soon.

## Inner Vision

This will be the year

I say goodbye to fear

I live right now and here

my vision true and clear

I'll let the drama go

I'll let the Dharma show

me how to let things flow

and see my garden grow

This will be the season

things happen for a reason

where conscious self-respect

sets up cause and effect

This will be the week

I let my own heart speak

I'll function at my peak

I am the one I seek


This will be the day

I mean each word I say

from morning until night

I'll walk the path of light


This will be the hour

I open as a flower

I grow into my power

accepting sweet and sour


This will be the minute

I honour what is in it

the beauty without limit

the stillness that's infinite

This will be the time

new openings align

coincidences rhyme

and we are in our prime


The world is your invention

so set a new intention

embarking on your mission

with perfect inner vision

*The teachings of the Buddha are known as the 'Dharma'. I am not a Buddhist, but it is a wisdom tradition that I find extremely helpful.*

# Acknowledgements

Thanks to everyone who helped to make this book possible, including:

Flloyd (with two els) Kennedy for helping me to navigate the intricacies of self-publishing.

Catherine Carroll for coming to one of my workshops, then publishing her book, which inspired me to get on with mine.

Jennie Wishart for the stunning illustrations and cover artwork.

Eddie Roberts for belief and philanthropy.

My mum for nurturing my fondness for words from an early age, with the wonderful books she chose for me and my sister.

# About the Author

Photo: Victor Krasowski

Tom George is a writer and musician based in Liverpool, UK. In addition to writing and performing, Tom runs writing and wellbeing workshops with community groups and literary festivals.
Tom has released has two CDs of original music and several poetry zines and pamphlets.
*Keys to the Forest* is his first 'proper' book.
www.tomgeorgearts.wordpress.com

Jennie Wishart - illustrator
www.instagram.com/jennie.wishart/

www.ingramcontent.com/pod-product-compliance
Lightning Source LLC
Chambersburg PA
CBHW042117100526
**44587CB00025B/4097**